Honoring the
WHOLE You

Everyday Work-Life Management Strategies
for Professional Moms and Caregivers

Honoring the WHOLE You

Everyday Work-Life Management Strategies for Professional Moms and Caregivers

DR. SHARLENE ALLEN-MILTON

2513 N. Rolling Rd.
P.O. Box 47343
Windsor Mill, MD 21244

phone: 443-470-9355

Ordering Information:
Quantity sales: special discounts are available on quantity purchases by corporations, associations, and others. For details, contact the publisher at the address above. Orders by U.S. trade bookstores and wholesalers.

Please contact Dr. Sharlene Allen-Milton:

Email:
dr.sharleneallenmilton@gmail.com

Website:
https://www.drsharleneallen.com/

Facebook:
https://www.Facebook.com/Askdrshar

Instagram:
https://www.instagram.com/drsharleneallen

ISBN: 978-0-578-87588-0

Thank you for taking this journey in the direction of more effective work-life management! I created an affirmation video that will help you cement the new habits you develop as you complete the exercises in this workbook.

Download the affirmations video at www.drsharleneallen.com

About the Author

Dr. Sharlene Allen-Milton, LCSW-C, CLC, also known as the "Work-Life Management Strategist," is a native of New York. She holds a Bachelor of Science degree in Social Work from Morgan State University, a Master of Clinical Social Work degree from Smith College, and a Doctor of Education degree in Human and Organizational Learning from George Washington University. Working as a clinical social worker with adults, children, and youth for over 18 years, Dr. Allen-Milton possesses a wealth of experience working with individuals experiencing social-emotional challenges.

Dr. Allen-Milton is a published author of peer-reviewed articles, her research interests are in the areas of dispersed/remote social work, and work-life management for professional and matriculating mothers. Dr. Allen-Milton has extensive experience providing personal and professional development workshops for human services workers, and mental health education to faith-based organizations. Dr. Allen-Milton serves as an Assistant Professor of Social Work at an Historically Black College and University (HBCU) in Maryland.

A defining moment in Dr. Allen-Milton's life was in 2016 when she was a new mother, a new faculty member, and planning to marry: that's when she personally became acquainted with work-life management. As a result of overcoming issues associated with work-life imbalance--lack of priority setting, self-doubt, anxiety, lack of organization--Dr. Allen-Milton decided to use her personal and educational experience to help professional moms and caregivers develop work-life harmony. Dr. Allen-Milton is a Christian, a wife, and the mother to one daughter. Whether in the role of mother, wife, professor, or coach, Dr. Allen-Milton's motto and method are "to educate, equip, and support people to their place of freedom."

Dedication

I dedicate this book
to professional moms and caregivers everywhere.

To my husband and daughter;
To my parents, siblings, family, and friends;
To my spiritual leaders of All Nations Worship
Assembly-Baltimore;

Thank you!

Table of Contents

Introduction

I am so excited that you have taken the step to manage work and life so that you can experience mental freedom and work-life harmony. I help professional moms and caregivers struggling with competing priorities in work and life. I count it a privilege and an honor that you are entrusting me to help facilitate you through this journey to work-life harmony.

Currently, I am a wife, mother, and Assistant Professor of Social Work at an HBCU in Maryland. I have over 18 years of clinical social work experience and my life's purpose is to educate, equip, and support people into their place of freedom.

I became a Work-Life Management Strategist as a result of personal and educational experiences. At 42, I had three major blessings in my life. The first was that I was new to motherhood. In August 2016, my daughter was 7 months old, I was getting married in 5 months, and I had just acquired a faculty job at a university in Maryland. Let's just say that "learning curve" and "transition" were understatements during this time.

I was struggling, silently crying because of self-doubt, anxiety and postpartum depression. I was mentally overwhelmed even while loving my new life. I needed strategies to help manage my new roles of mom, faculty member, and wife. I was constantly praying and asking myself, "How do women manage work and life?"

In January 2017, God heard my cry. On the second day of attending a faith-based leadership conference hosted by my church, I felt stressed. The speaker discerned this and prayed for me. One of the things that she instructed me to do was to be refreshed in God's presence daily. It would give me the grace to do all that I needed to do. That divine encounter allowed me to truly understand that I am able to manage my work and life, not through my finite strength, but by tapping into God's grace daily.

For five years now, I have personally experienced, researched, written articles, and presented several workshops on the topic of Work-Life Management. This has allowed me to acquire work-life management solutions geared toward overcoming the mental overwhelm that accompanies the competing priorities of being a professional, mom, or caregiver, and experience the mental freedom that comes with work-life harmony. I want to help you do the same.

This workbook uses my Educate, Equip, and Support (EES) Method.

The EES Method is designed to:

- Educate you on the foundations of work-life management.

- Equip you with work-life management strategies.

- Assist you in applying work-life concepts to practical life.

- Provide support by teaching you how to cultivate a lifestyle of self-care.

- Support you by offering journal prompts specifically crafted to assist you in uncovering, at a deep level, what impedes your mental freedom and work-life harmony.

As you utilize this workbook here's what you can expect:

- To understand the difference between work-life balance and work-life management.

- To gain specific work-life management strategies to apply to your everyday life.

- To become a practitioner of self-care.

- To gain a deeper understanding of yourself.

- Through journaling, you will gain the mental clarity and freedom needed to execute strategies learned as you experience work-life harmony.

Congratulations on your decision to take this journey!

Educate

Let's Build Your Foundation

What is Work-Life Balance?

As early as the mid-nineteenth century, history portrayed work as gender specific. Men worked outside of the home and women were viewed as caretakers of children and the home. Due to women advocacy campaigns, there was a dramatic increase of women in the workforce during the 1930-1970s. As a result of more women entering the workforce -- of which 40% were married women -- the notion of work-life balance began to gain more momentum, particularly in the 1960s (Allenman et al., 2018; Davies & Frank, 2014).

Today, there is evidence that there has been a shift in that narrative as it relates to professional moms and caregivers. According to the Bureau of Labor and Statistics report for 2019, 66.4 % of professional mothers have a child or children younger than 6, while those with a child or children age 6 to 17 was 76.8 %. That's a huge increase of professional moms in the workplace since the 1960s. Professional mothers and caregivers are now leaders of companies and even serving as Vice President of the United States!

Although professional mothers have made great strides, what is often not heard is her story, her narrative. There are aspects of the life domain for professional moms and caregivers of color that are overlooked and not explicitly taken into account in the work-life balance discussion. In addition to work and family, many professional moms and caregivers also manage aspects of life associated with race, spirituality, and being a caregiver to immediate and extended family. This is not usually discussed in the majority of conversations about work-life balance.

Work-life balance is a critical area of concern for women of color in the academy, traditional work, remote/dispersed work, and entrepreneurial work (Ahmad, 2014; Jung & Heppner, 2014; Kamenou, 2008; Wang, 2015).

Employed mothers hold multiple spaces and identities simultaneously. Many mothers are the sole, majority, or contributing source of income to their nuclear and extended family, whether they are domestic or abroad. They are also cultivators and caregivers to their children, parents, extended family or fictive kin. They are part of an interconnected community of support to family, friends and civic organizations (Alleman, Allen-Milton, Darrell and Vakalahi, 2018).

Journal

What is the story you wish people knew about you?

_____

_____

_____

_____

_____

_____

_____

_____

_____

_____

_____

_____

What are the multiple spaces and identities that you operate in that need attention?

_____

_____

_____

_____

_____

_____

_____

_____

_____

_____

_____

_____

_____

Theoretical Lens: A Womanist Perspective

I wear glasses. It helps me see the world effectively. So, too, is the purpose of a theoretical framework. A theoretical framework sets the foundation for the lens from which we view a given topic or concept. The theoretical lens that guides my work is from a womanist perspective. A womanist perspective highlights and normalizes the character essence of a woman as she shows up in the world.

Historically, the female voice has been authenticated through talking or storytelling. By culture, we are storytellers. We use proverbs, affirmations, idioms, scripture, lyrics, and whatever is deemed essential for the knowledge to be conveyed. This promotes community building and simultaneously functions as a point of resistance through counter storytelling (Phillips, 2006).

According to Alice Walker, a "womanist perspective emphasizes three key themes: 1) the meaning of self-definition and self-valuation which challenges stereotypes, resists oppression, and strengthens collectivity and relationships; 2) the importance of naming and claiming culture; and 3) the interlocking multiple oppressions that impact women of color." (Alleman, Allen-Milton, Darrell, & Vakalahi, p.2018). Dr. Melissa Littlefield builds on this perspective and suggests that African-American women have an environmental niche in response to various forms of oppression, which are adaptation strategies inclusive of: workers outside the home; nurturer-provider role strength; economic independence; self-reliance; autonomy; religiosity which unites self to religious beliefs; socio-emotional support; social support -- kinship networks, family, and close friends (Littlefield, 2003). This framework allows for a more holistic view when engaging in work-life management discussions.

Journal

What about this passage resonates with you as it relates to your identity?

_____

_____

_____

_____

_____

_____

_____

_____

_____

_____

_____

Are there any stereotypical, or negative narratives that you would like to change? How will you do that?

_____

_____

_____

_____

_____

_____

_____

_____

_____

_____

_____

_____

_____

Who are you and what parts of yourself have you been ignoring?

_____

_____

_____

_____

_____

_____

_____

_____

_____

_____

_____

_____

_____

Work-Life Management

In the work-life balance chapter I gave its history and its progression. In this chapter, I share my view on why I do not not believe in work-life balance. I prefer the term "work-life management." Here's why:

Have you ever taken a look at the vintage picture of balanced scales? Lady Justice is the perfect image that comes to mind. She is blindfolded, holding scales that appear equally distributed or balanced. Have you ever experienced jury-duty? They don't ask if you can be balanced regarding the court issue, they ask if you can be NEUTRAL. Lady justice is not blind and balanced, she is blind and neutral regarding the cases presented to her.

Professional mothers and caregivers on a daily basis deal with work responsibilities, spousal, domestic and caregiving duties, along with volunteering in extracurricular activities for self and child(ren). It would be mentally stressful to think that this could be balanced. As professional women and caregivers we are trying to live up to this falsehood of balancing our various identities and domains -- self, wife, mother, professional, committee member, and the list can go on and on.

We will never be able to balance our various identities and domains because there isn't a 50/50 split between them. When I became a new mom, professor, and wife, I interviewed other professional moms that were married on how to balance work and life. Their responses were resoundingly the same: you can't balance your various identities and domains, they have to be managed. Some days this area will get 10%, another area will get 10%, another will get 20% and another will get 60%. Depending on the day and what has to get accomplished, the percentages and your management of the domains will change. The TRUTH is we have to manage our various roles and domains.

Journal

How were you trying to balance work and life?

_____

_____

_____

_____

_____

_____

_____

_____

_____

_____

_____

_____

What kind of stressors did you experience trying to balance work and life?

_____

_____

_____

_____

_____

_____

_____

_____

_____

_____

_____

_____

What occurred within upon hearing you no longer have to balance work and life but manage them?

_____

_____

_____

_____

_____

_____

_____

_____

_____

_____

_____

_____

Work-Life Harmony Defined

Work-life harmony doesn't involve perfection. Neither does it involve two scales being equally distributed, that is neutrality. Work-life harmony is like an orchestra. An orchestra has different musical sections, but may sound out of sync or out of harmony when they are individually rehearsing their part of a musical score. However, each section is interdependent, so when played together they produce a beautiful, harmonized piece. Work-life harmony involves the perception of efficacy and satisfaction in work and family roles that are in alignment with life values. Work and life are not in competition with each other, they are interdependent. This requires management of the various roles and identities of daily existence (Greenhouse and Allen, 2011). Work and life harmony involves interdependency in order for work-life harmony to be achieved.

Journal

Have you ever perceived your work and life to be interdependent?

_____

_____

_____

_____

_____

_____

_____

_____

_____

_____

_____

How are they interdependent?

_____

_____

_____

_____

_____

_____

_____

_____

_____

_____

_____

_____

_____

What in your work and life do you feel need to be managed?

_____

_____

_____

_____

_____

_____

_____

_____

_____

_____

_____

_____

What needs to be done differently as it relates to work and life?

_____

_____

_____

_____

_____

_____

_____

_____

_____

_____

_____

_____

_____

_____

Stress

Stress can come from any event or thought that makes you feel emotionally frustrated, angry, or nervous. Stress can also show up as tension in your physical body. Whether stress shows up emotionally or physically it is your body's way of responding to a challenge or demand. According to Dr. Caroline Leaf, mental health and cognitive neuroscientist, stress can cause issues with digestion, cloudy thinking, and fluctuating mood levels that range from low to high energy levels.

Oftentimes, as professional moms and caregivers, we struggle with managing aspects of work and life. As a result, we experience stress due to competing priorities. Having to attend the important evening meeting -- but first make dinner, and ensure that your child does homework, eats dinner and takes a bath, and gets settled before the meeting -- can all be stressful. Constantly being on the go without engaging in self-care can cause feelings of overwhelm.

In addition to domestic and caretaking responsibilities, work can feel all-consuming and seem so overwhelming that your version of "taking a moment" is crying in the bathroom or at bedtime. Other signs of stress are headaches, backaches, feelings of fatigue, isolation, and lack of interest in things that used to give you pleasure. These signs are an SOS for help in the area of work-life management. In my work as a clinical social worker and therapist, I have seen where undealt with stress lays the foundation for anxiety and depression.

Journal

What areas in your life are causing you stress?

_____

_____

_____

_____

_____

_____

_____

_____

_____

_____

_____

What event or thought concerning your work-life domains (nurturer, provider, community social supporter) is causing you to feel frustrated, fatigued, angry, overwhelmed or nervous?

_____

_____

_____

_____

_____

_____

_____

_____

_____

_____

_____

_____

What work-life challenge or demand is your body responding to?

_____

_____

_____

_____

_____

_____

_____

_____

_____

_____

_____

_____

_____

What work-life challenge would you like help managing?

_____

_____

_____

_____

_____

_____

_____

_____

_____

_____

_____

_____

_____

_____

Equip

Work-Life Management Strategies

Self-Worth

Leading motivational speaker Tom Bilyeu defines mindset as a set of beliefs of what is possible in life. He also says that one's mindset determines quality of life. An aspect of mindset is our self-worth. One of the things I teach in my Self-Worth Intensive Program is that our mindset can be one that is rigid or one that is expansive. Dr. Carlo Dweck, mindset expert, suggested that there are two types of mindsets, fixed and growth. A fixed mindset is one that is unmoving, believing that the ability to change is limited. A growth mindset, on the other hand, is a mindset that looks at challenges and obstacles, personal and professional, as learning opportunities to build capacity.

According to positive psychology, self-worth is the manner in which we esteem or value ourselves. It is grounded in sober self-awareness, knowledge of strengths and weaknesses, forgiveness, and the ability to combat negative identity messaging. A self-worth mindset that is grounded in positivity and optimism is critical to achieving work and life harmony.

Leveling up on self-worth means that it is possible to come from behind the curtain of self-doubt and stand center stage, embracing the things you do well despite what others think. It also involves saying good-bye to self-comparison. Lastly, it involves remembering the track record of when you were supported by God and your tribe which helped bring you through stressful situations. It is positive self-worth that sets the foundation for a willingness to set boundaries, have hard conversations, and valuing self-enough to be loved and respected by self and others in the workplace and in life.

Journal

What was your mindset concerning self-worth?

_____

_____

_____

_____

_____

_____

_____

_____

_____

_____

_____

_____

How has that mindset changed? Write, "I express self-worth in the following ways…"

_____

_____

_____

_____

_____

_____

_____

_____

_____

_____

_____

_____

_____

_____

How do you think you can improve your self-worth?

_____

_____

_____

_____

_____

_____

_____

_____

_____

_____

_____

_____

_____

What are you willing to do to grow in the area of self-worth?

_____

_____

_____

_____

_____

_____

_____

_____

_____

_____

_____

_____

_____

Combating Negative Self-Messaging

An area of self-worth that is resistant to a growth mindset is negative self-messaging. Negative self-messages are internal or external narratives that play and replay in our minds that are opposite from our true identity. Negative self-messaging can adversely impact work and life as they are a breeding ground for self-doubt, low self-worth, anxiety, depression, and feeling stuck. But there is hope! Dr. Caroline Leaf says if the negative thoughts can be wired into the brain, they can be wired out of the brain. Here are four ways to combat negative self-messaging:

- Be conscious of where and how negative self-messaging emerges.
- Be aware of the thoughts and beliefs that occur when negative self-messages show up. Ask yourself if the negative self-messages are true or false?
- Challenge your negative self-messaging by being more loving and kind to yourself.
- Change your negative thoughts with declarations and affirmations.

Journal

What negative self-messages do you experience?

_____

_____

_____

_____

_____

_____

_____

_____

_____

_____

_____

What is the impact of your negative self-messages on work and or life?

_____

_____

_____

_____

_____

_____

_____

_____

_____

_____

_____

_____

Affirmations

Affirmations are a powerful weapon to combating negative self-messaging as they cancel the lie and the torment of the negative message by stating the truth. Affirmations are effective tools for the workplace and life. An affirmation is a declaration of what you want to occur. One of my foundational spiritual beliefs is that "life and death are in the power of the tongue," Proverbs 18:21. As a result, we can proclaim life over ourselves or proclaim things that can keep us stuck. Affirmations, if properly created, have a profound impact on the conscious, subconscious, and unconscious parts of the brain. They can also cause things to materialize or manifest.

I learned the supernatural power of declarations from my spiritual leader, Yolanda Stith, also known as The Praying Apostle. In her book, *Invisible Battlegrounds: Winning the War in the Body, Mind, and Spiritual Realm*, as well as her "Prayer School: Boosted," Apostle Stith explains the power of declarations so eloquently. She says, "When one makes a decree it activates supernatural motion to take place. Your words work for or against you and give permission (good or bad) to live in your life."

Affirmations activate a bi-directional relationship between you and God. Affirmations also have the power to change you and your surroundings. When stating or creating affirmations it is important that you own the words used to create the affirmation. Generic affirmations do not work as well as affirmations that were created by you, for you, and resonate within you. Believe that it will come to pass. Affirmations support you when you are not feeling your best and subconsciously carry you from a fixed to a growth mindset. Remember that when you decree a thing it shall be established (Job 28:28)!

Journal

List five to ten affirmations or declarations that cancel either negative identity messaging or self-comparison. As you compose your affirmations it is important that your remember these suggestions:

1. Affirm in present tense.
2. Affirm using only positive wording. Affirm what you want, not what you don't want.
3. Be brief.
4. Be specific.
5. Use a verb ending with –ing.
6. Use one emotion or feeling word.
7. Make affirmations for yourself, not others.

Examples of affirmations:

- I am loved
- I am enough
- I am attracting relationships, resources, and opportunities for my next level

Example of an improper affirmation:

- I will no longer engage in self comparison, instead I will engage in self-affirmation

For more information please see affirmations video.

What's Important: Priorities

Have you ever experienced being reactionary to people, places and/ or things that you shouldn't have been because your priorities weren't established? Lack of priorities can cause many to fall into people pleasing because we struggle with wanting to be liked and accepted (I digress, a topic for another time). According to Webster's Dictionary, a priority is a moral, value, concern, or desire that comes before all others.

When we don't have priorities, the various identities and domains that we are involved in can feel like they're in competition with each other. This doesn't have to be so. An aspect of work-life management is knowing your priorities. This can be established by the following:

1. Write down your main priorities as it pertains to life and work.
2. Be still and check in with God and ask if there are people, places, or things that you have made priorities that you shouldn't have. Trust me, an answer will come. For me, checking in with God is a non-negotiable as that is where I get my wisdom, clarity and direction from.
3. It is imperative that you are aware of the order of importance of your priorities. For example, if family comes before work and you are home on the computer working on a project (outside of work hours) and your child comes to you with a request right at the peak of your work zone, feelings of frustration should be minimal because you're clear about your priorities -- family comes first.

Keep in mind that priorities will be different from person to person, and that's okay. It is important to take time to reflect on what is important to you in the area of work and life. As those priorities become clear, they set the stage for establishing boundaries.

Journal

How have you been responding or reacting to people, places, and things because of lack of priorities?

_____

_____

_____

_____

_____

_____

_____

_____

_____

_____

_____

_____

_____

What are your thoughts about taking the time to be still to think about your priorities?

_____

_____

_____

_____

_____

_____

_____

_____

_____

_____

_____

_____

What are your priorities for work, home and life?

_____

_____

_____

_____

_____

_____

_____

_____

_____

_____

_____

_____

_____

What are competing factors, if any, with your now established priorities (please refer to this question when we get to the section on boundaries)?

_____

_____

_____

_____

_____

_____

_____

_____

_____

_____

_____

_____

Boundaries

Many stress manifestations could be managed by boundaries. Webster Dictionary defines boundaries as a line that marks the limits of an area. Drs. Henry Cloud and John Townsend suggest that boundaries allow for freedom and responsibility. They also posit that boundaries serve two functions. The first is they define who we are and who we are not. The second is that boundaries safeguard us by keeping the good in and the unacceptable out. Boundaries, based on their function, protect us from mental, physical, emotional, and psychological stressors or triggers. Boundaries also show others how we would like to be treated.

I challenge you to think about situations where you have established boundaries in place and situations where you don't have established boundaries in place, and why. Sometimes boundaries need to be established with ourselves. An example of this is saying you will do something, and for whatever reason, it does not get done. Why is that? We need to deem ourselves a priority and important enough to keep and maintain our boundaries.

Hard Conversations

When establishing boundaries there are times when you may need to have what may seem like a hard conversation with others at work and in life. At work, boundaries may need to be set regarding responding to communications after work hours. At home, boundaries may need to be set regarding a sleep schedule. It may seem like a hard conversation because the other party may be used to interacting with you in one way and you desire to change and set boundaries regarding that interaction. As I write this I am smiling because I remember being such a "yes/ sure" person that when I said "No," the response was a chuckle and "Stop playing." When boundaries are set and people see that you are not budging, your boundaries will be respected.

When we establish boundaries, our stress levels decrease because we are no longer emotionally upset doing things that we really don't want to do. We no longer feel bad because we didn't speak up when we had the opportunity. Remember, "No" is a complete sentence.

Journal

What does it feel like when boundaries have been violated?

_____

_____

_____

_____

_____

_____

_____

_____

_____

_____

_____

What does it feel it like when boundaries haven't been enforced?

_____

_____

_____

_____

_____

_____

_____

_____

_____

_____

_____

_____

_____

What does it feel like when boundaries have been enforced?

_____

_____

_____

_____

_____

_____

_____

_____

_____

_____

_____

_____

_____

How do you feel about having hard conversations?

_____

_____

_____

_____

_____

_____

_____

_____

_____

_____

_____

_____

_____

_____

Do you welcome it or shy away from it?

_____

_____

_____

_____

_____

_____

_____

_____

_____

_____

_____

_____

_____

Set Goals

According to Webster's dictionary, goals are what you aspire to accomplish or achieve in a given time. Setting goals involves knowing your priorities. Some people have daily, weekly, monthly and annual goals. Others set goals based on the demands of their career, while others have daily goals based on the needs of the family.

A recent goal for me was writing this book. Because my priorities are God, family, self-care, work, and church, I had to create writing goals with my priorities in mind. The publisher had given me a draft deadline, so I had a conversation with my immediate family. They were in full support. My five year old daughter was so proud of her mommy that when it was writing time she would use her pretend computer to write her book or pretend to teach on self-worth. It was amazing to see my influence through the eyes of my daughter.

I often used the weekend and Mondays to do a lot of writing. During the time I wrote this book, I ordered takeout for the family way more than I should have, but I was able to meet two goals: feeding my family and writing my book. There were some weekends that my husband cooked, of which I was so grateful for his act of service to help me meet my goal.

Many of us may consider goal setting in one area of the work, home, life domains, but may not be as diligent in creating goals in other aspects of the work, home, life, domains. As a professional mom, we are goal oriented with our careers and family, but we forget ourselves. My challenge to you is to create a goal for yourself that you desire to accomplish in addition to your career and family goals. Please see the journal section for more details.

Journal

Anxiety Canada's PDF '*Guide for Goal Setting*' provides a simple, but effective guide on how to identify, set, and achieve realistic goals. When engaging in this activity you will get the maximum experience if you pay attention to each domain separately -- work, home, and life -- and make sure to include smaller goals for each domain as well.

The full guide is available as a PDF download. The link is in the resource section.

Here are 5 recommended steps to goal setting:

1. Identify your goals with a focus on being realistic and specific.
2. Break down these goals into smaller steps.
3. Identify potential obstacles between you and your goals.
4. Build a schedule and allow adequate time to pursue goals.
5. Do it!

How do you feel about setting goals for the various domains that you are involved in?

_____

_____

_____

_____

_____

_____

_____

_____

_____

_____

_____

_____

What are your goals for work, home, and life? Remember that goals should be specific and realistic to each domain.

_____

_____

_____

_____

_____

_____

_____

_____

_____

_____

_____

_____

What are your hard stop times?

_____

_____

_____

_____

_____

_____

_____

_____

_____

_____

_____

_____

_____

_____

_____

How will you track the progress?

_____

_____

_____

_____

_____

_____

_____

_____

_____

_____

_____

Get Organized

Getting organized involves strategies -- setting priorities, setting goals, creating a schedule, keeping track of time -- that are aligned with your body rhythm and your personality. If body rhythm is most optimal at 3:00 p.m., waking up at 5:00 a.m. and attempting to accomplish goals may just be a waste of time. The converse is also true. If you are most optimal at 5:00 a.m., don't wait until 6:00 p.m. to accomplish work because it will be an uphill battle. The bottom line is this: find out what time of the day your ability to get work done is at its peak and knock out tasks, goals, prepping and planning!

One of the things that I have learned on this work-life management journey is that getting organized is subjective. When getting organized, it is important not to compare your insides to other people's outsides because organization looks different for everyone. Many of us try organization strategies based on an implementation plan of a person whose personality is totally different than our own. When these strategies fail, they don't make us feel good about ourselves or our abilities. Many organization strategies are from a white male perspective and excludes the multiple roles that include parenting, caretaking, selfcare, and working.

Don't get me wrong, you can gain a lot of tips from people who are different from you. But at the end of the day, what organization looks like for you, especially according to your work-life domains, may not look the same for another, and that's okay. Below are some organization resources for different personality types -- those who struggle with structure and those that welcome a structured environment!

- *Atomic Habits: Tiny Changes, Remarkable Results: An Easy & Proven Way To Build Good Habits & Break Bad Ones* by James Clear
- *Purge with Passion: Organizing Principles from a Christian Perspective* by Jodie Watson
- *Life Management for Busy Women* by Elizabeth George

Due to the high level of subjectivity that is associated with organization, I also provide work-life management audits in this area. These are the type of questions I ask my clients:

- Do you struggle with structure or do you thrive and strive in it?
- What times of the day do you feel most optimal?
- Would you like to create goals around the time you are feeling most optimal?

Journal

What happened when you tried to apply organization strategies based on the implementation plan of a person whose personality was totally different than yours?

_____

_____

_____

_____

_____

_____

_____

_____

_____

_____

What is your rhythm? What times of the day or night are you optimal?

_____

_____

_____

_____

_____

_____

_____

_____

_____

_____

_____

_____

_____

What does organization look like for you?

_____

_____

_____

_____

_____

_____

_____

_____

_____

_____

_____

_____

_____

_____

Support

Self-Care

Seven Domains of Self-Care

When I engaged in a Google search on self-care, I often saw images of women with towels wrapped around their heads and mud masks on their faces. While that is one dimension of self-care, there are several others that need focus and attention. According to the University of Maryland, there are eight dimensions of self-care. Self-care is multi-faceted and should be viewed as a priority. Self-care involves engaging in mindful, conscientious actions to embrace physical, mental/ intellectual, social, emotional, spiritual, and financial well-being.

The various self-care domains may seem many, but my intention is not to stress you, but to make you aware of the various domains and allow you to choose which ones you need to work on. Here are seven self-care domains I recommend you consider. Some of these self-care domains may require an investment. You are worth it!

Physical

This domain involves embracing the value of health conscious activities. The physical aspect of self-care attends to your body and ensures that you have adequate rest, nutrition, healthcare, and exercise. Examples of physical self-care are: getting proper rest, ensuring 6-8 hours of sleep; hiring a nutritionist to create individualized meals to ensure that you are getting all of the nutrients your body needs; making necessary doctors' appointments to maximize your health; being physically active for 30 min at least four days a week (if that is too overwhelming start at 15 mins and work your way up from there).

Mental/Intellectual

The mental and intellectual domain concentrates on the importance of creating or finding opportunities for mental stimulation for the purposes of learning, creating, and critical thinking. In sum, the focus of mental/intellectual self-care is lifelong learning. Listening to a podcast of interest, taking an online class, or hosting a Zoom discussion on a particular topic are some ways to engage in mental/intellectual stimulation.

Spiritual

While the physical, mental/intellectual, emotional, financial and communal self-care domains prioritize ways to improve the body, soul, mind, will, and emotions, the spiritual domain centers on the third part of your tri-part being, the spirit. This domain allows for a bi-directional flow and relationship between you and God. This flow can be obtained through prayer, by attending a faith-based institution, by reading the Bible, or in stillness. Prioritizing this domain often results in an increased sense of peace, clarity, wisdom, direction, and comfort.

Emotional

This self-care domain gives attention to your worth, esteem, and sense of acceptance. Emotional self-care is needed especially in times of stress, adversity, and the need to be realistic about a situation. This domain can be actualized by hanging out with friends and family, engaging in community (which I will be talk about later in this chapter), or seeing a therapist or a coach.

Financial

I remember watching Michael Jordan on the Oprah Winfrey show where she asked him about living on a budget. He responded, "My mother said, 'No matter how much money you have, you always budget.'" The financial domain highlights the importance of financial literacy. Self-care as it pertains to our financial wellness allows us to embrace our relationship with money. Financial self-care also allows us to live by a budget, which allows us to make sensible financial decisions, live within our means, and prepare for short and long range goals and emergencies. This domain can be achieved by taking a financial literacy class, listening to Dave Ramsey's podcasts, adopting Dave Ramsey's baby steps (see resource section), or hiring a financial coach.

Finding Your Community

Finding your community is essential to self-care and work-life management. Communities help to hold space for whatever you need. Community comes in various forms, such as groups, tribes, rooms for the purposes to educate, equip, and uplift you emotionally or mentally. There are several types of communities, including social emotional communities, support communities, and support systems.

- **Social emotional communities** - These allow for mutual reciprocity in allowing a person to feel valued and cared for. You feel safe to be vulnerable. There are also communities that provide support, and they, too, come in different forms. Those forms are as follows:
- **Specific need communities** - These provide for a specific need (food, money, shelter)

- **Emotional support communities** - These provide nurturance and validation. Examples of these are your sister circles.
- **Organizational support communities** - These are churches, civic organizations, recreation centers, and fraternities and sororities.

Many of us may feel mentally, physically, and/or emotionally overwhelmed in the workplace because we do not use or take the time to know what benefits are available to us. Look into your benefits package and, if you feel stressed out, ask HR (Human Resources) about taking time off using Employee Assistance Benefits. See what self-care domains apply to your flexible spending account and use it. You could have opportunities that you're passing up on because of lack of knowledge. Know and discuss your work options as you may be able to get time off when you need it.

Journal

How have you put self-care on the backburner?

_____

_____

_____

_____

_____

_____

_____

_____

_____

_____

Which self-care domain could use more of your focus?

_____

_____

_____

_____

_____

_____

_____

_____

_____

_____

_____

_____

_____

How will you make incorporating the needed self-care domains in your life a priority?

_____

_____

_____

_____

_____

_____

_____

_____

_____

_____

_____

_____

Control and the Power of Surrender

How many of us have challenges with control? We can't control everything, but we can control the things we can change and ask for wisdom for the things that we can't (serenity prayer). When we try to control things, it is our ego that doesn't want to be bruised, or wants to feel good, or feel perfect. Perfectionism can often be tied to reasons for control, which is often rooted in past issues that cause a strong need to appear perfect and all put together. Culture and media have also painted a false picture, and that picture for many of us, is in our subconscious. What picture am I referring to? The one projecting that we have to be supermom. Supermom is probably crying in the bathroom or when she goes to sleep because supermom isn't real.

Can I just pop that bubble and say that it's okay to not have it all together? I remember when I became a mom, wife, and faculty member, I struggled with control as I was trying to be the best wife, mom, and professor. I was trying to have it all together. It's okay to make mistakes.

Control is rooted in lack of trust. We think that everything will go to hell in a handbasket if we are not leading it, or if our hand is not in it. That simply isn't true. It's okay for you not to be in control of everything. I liken control to a delusion that we are directors in a play telling people what to do, how to or not to act, how to behave, etc. Then we get upset when they choose not to follow our directives! Isn't that funny? People have the power of choice.

We are finite. We have limitations. There are times that we will hit the mark regarding boundaries, self-care, parenting, saying affirmations, working, priorities, and organizations -- and some days we won't. I had to learn this in order to have peace with myself. To obtain wisdom for my family, work, and daily living, I had to surrender to an infinite source. I am talking about surrendering to God.

Surrender takes humbling ourselves and seeking God for the answers. James 1:5 says if any of you lack wisdom, ask. Surrender also involves vulnerability to ask for help. During a quiet time of your choosing, you can simply say, "God I am struggling with _____ . You said if anyone lacks wisdom to ask. I am asking for your wisdom as it relates to _____ . Show me your answer." Look for the answers, they will come. Remember, with all that we do, we can't pour from an empty cup.

Journal

What aspects of your life do you try to control to your detriment?

_____

_____

_____

_____

_____

_____

_____

_____

_____

_____

How has this <u>not</u> worked for you?

_____

_____

_____

_____

_____

_____

_____

_____

_____

_____

_____

_____

_____

_____

What are aspects of your life that you are willing to surrender?

_____

_____

_____

_____

_____

_____

_____

_____

_____

_____

_____

_____

_____

_____

How will you surrender to God areas that you have tried to control?

_____

_____

_____

_____

_____

_____

_____

_____

_____

_____

_____

_____

_____

Resources

Educate

Alleman, A. S., Milton, S. A., Darrell, L., & Vakalahi, H. F. O. (2018). "Women of Color and Work–Life Balance in an Urban Environment: What Is Reality?" In *Urban Social Work*, 2(1), 80-95.

Greenhaus, J. & Allen, T.D. (2011). "Work-Family Balance Review and Extension of the Literature." In *Handbook of Occupational Health Psychology*, 2, 165-183.

Littlefield, M. B. (2003). "A Womanist Perspective For Social Work With African American Women." In *Social Thought*, 22(4), 3-17.

Phillips, L. (Ed.). (2006). *the Womanist Reader*. Taylor & Francis.

Equip

Anxiety Canada's PDF *Guide for Goal Setting.* (n.d.). https://www. anxietycanada.com/sites/default/files/GoalSetting.pdf

Bilyeu, T. (2020). https://university.impacttheory.com/mindset101

Clear, J. (2018). *Atomic Habits: Tiny Changes, Remarkable Results: An Easy and Proven Way To Build Good Habits and Break Bad Ones.* Avery.

Cloud, H., & Townsend, J. (2017). *Boundaries Updated and Expanded Edition: When to Say Yes, How to Say No To Take Control of Your Life.* Zondervan.

Dweck, C. S. (2008). *Mindset: The New Psychology Of Success.* Random House Digital, Inc.

George, E. (2014). *Life Management for Busy Women.* Harvest House Publishers.

Holy Bible: The Message (the Bible in contemporary language). 2005. Colorado Springs, CO: NavPress.

Leaf, C. (2020). 3 Signs your Body Is In Toxic Stress and What You Can Do About It. https://drleaf.com/blogs/news/3-signs-your-body-is-in-toxic-stress-and-what-you-can-do-about-it

Stevenson, M. (2019). *Abba: Experience God as Father and Redeem Your Failure, Hurt, and Pain.* Charisma House.

Stith, Y. (2019). *Invisible Battlegrounds: Winning the War on the Body, Mind, and Spiritual Realm.* Destiny Image Publishers, Inc.

Watson, J. (2013). *Purge with Passion: Organizing Principles from a Christian Perspective.* Westbow Press.

Support

Dimensions of Wellness, (UMD) University of Maryland's Your Guide to Living Well. [Last accessed March 2020]. Available from: https://umwellness.wordpress.com/8-dimensions-of-wellness/

Financial

Dave Ramsey's 7 Baby Steps. https://www.daveramsey.com/dave-ramsey-7-baby-steps

Dawn Robinson - The Money Phd. www.themoneyphd.com

References

Alleman, A. S., Milton, S. A., Darrell, L., & Vakalahi, H. F. O. (2018). "Women of Color and Work–Life Balance in an Urban Environment: What Is Reality?" In *Urban Social Work*, *2*(1), 80-95.

Bilyeu, T. (2020) https://university.impacttheory.com/mindset101

Bureau of Labor Statistics, "Employment Characteristics of Families Summary." (2020) https://www.bls.gov/news.release/famee.nr0.htm

Bureau of Labor Statistics, "Table 3: Employment Status of the Civilian Noninstitutional   Population by Age, Sex, and Race," *Current Population Survey* (2020).

Clear, J. (2018). *Atomic Habits: Tiny Changes, Remarkable Results: An Easy and Proven Way To Build Good Habits and Break Bad Ones.* Avery.

Cloud, H., & Townsend, J. (2017). *Boundaries, Updated and Expanded Edition: When to Say Yes, How to Say No To Take Control of Your Life.* Zondervan.

Dimensions of Wellness, (UMD) University of Maryland's Your Guide to Living Well. [Last accessed March, 1 2021]. Available from: https://umwellness.wordpress.com/8- dimensions-of-wellness/

Dweck, C. S. (2008). *Mindset: The New Psychology Of Success.* Random House Digital, Inc.

George, E. (2014). *Life Management for Busy Women.* Harvest House Publishers.

Greenhaus, J. & Allen, T.D. (2011). "Work-Family Balance: A Review and Extension of the Literature." In *Handbook of Occupational Health Psychology*, 2, 165-183.

Holy Bible: The Message (the Bible in contemporary language). 2005. Colorado Springs, CO: NavPress.

Leaf, C. (2020). 3 Signs your body is in toxic stress. https://drleaf.com/blogs/news/3-signs-your-body-is-in-toxic-stress-and-what-you-can-do-about-it

Littlefield, M. B. (2003). "A Womanist Perspective for Social Work with African American Women." In *Social Thought*, *22*(4), 3-17.

Merriam-Webster's Collegiate Dictionary (10th ed.). (1999). Merriam-Webster Incorporated.

Phillips, L. (Ed.). (2006). *the Womanist Reader*. Taylor & Francis.

Stith, Y, (2019) *Invisible Battlegrounds: Winning the War on the Body, Mind, and Spiritual Realm.* Destiny Image Publishers, Inc.

Taylor, S. E. (2011). "Social Support: A Review. In H. S. Friedman (Ed.)." In *The Oxford Handbook Of Health Psychology* (pp. 189–214). New York, NY: Oxford University Press.

Watson, J. (2013). *Purge with Passion: Organizing Principles from a Christian Perspective.* Westbow Press.

www.ingramcontent.com/pod-product-compliance
Lightning Source LLC
Chambersburg PA
CBHW062050090426

42740CB00016B/3080